Spin Your
WEB

Published by Waterfront Digital Press

2055 Oxford Avenue

Cardiff, CA 92007

ISBN 978-1-939116-16-1

Spin Your WEB

HOW TO BRAND YOURSELF
FOR SUCCESSFUL
ONLINE DATING

Damona Hoffman

Known as Dear Mrs D, Columnist and Radio Personality

TABLE OF CONTENTS

ACKNOWLEDGEMENTS

Eight years ago when I polished my first profile, I never thought it would become such a big part of my life. I was just trying to help out a heartbroken family member who wanted to find love. Many years and many profiles later I still thought it was just a hobby when my aunt Cecily encouraged me to do it professionally. She sent me my first client and I have not looked back. Thank you Todd, Eric and Jeff for being my guinea pigs in the early years. The beautiful relationships that you have found inspire me every day to keep doing this.

Thank you to my mother for always encouraging me to go after what I want and reminding me that I never have to settle for less than the best. I appreciate you being the biggest supporter and most difficult client I've ever had.

I'm also so thankful for the people that helped bring this book to life: Natasha Lewin, Kenneth Kales, Bill Gladstone and of course Barry Krost who believed in me when Dear Mrs D was just an idea. Jacquie Jordan, thank you for seeing my potential and promoting me back when there was nothing yet to promote. Mechelle and Kevin, thank you for your vision and belief that this is just the beginning.

To my Hollys—I love you both like sisters and through all our relationships, transitions, challenges and triumphs you've both always been there for me.

Adelaide Rose, I am so grateful to have a daughter like you who has taught me to always "just try." With you I've found my inner child again and I've been reminded that life is not measured by accomplishments, but by the quality of your time and the people you spent it with.

Last but not least, thank you to my wonderful husband, Seth, whose support made this all possible. You were my very first investor, editor and true love.

INTRODUCTION

We do practically everything online these days: chat with loved ones, map out directions for get-togethers with friends, shop for personal items. So why does meeting someone special have to be any different? Sounds reasonable enough, but with so many options out there, finding the right one can seem overwhelming.

One way to deal with these feelings is to ask yourself what makes you connect with a product online? Perhaps it has a great marketing campaign. This would equate to a friend introducing you to another friend of theirs to date. Or maybe you already know exactly what you're looking for so you Google it. This is like seeking out someone single on Facebook. But when you need something specific, you're more likely to go to a specific website that would carry that product and search for additional details to help inform your selection. You browse additional pictures of it, check out its statistics, maybe read a review and see what other people are saying about it. Generally you'll have a specific strategy to find the item you want. You'll go to the right site, make sure it's what you want and that you're getting it for the right price.

This made total sense to me when shopping online. Yet, when

I started dating online I had no idea how to sort through the mass of people and information to find who or what I was looking for.

At the time I began online dating, I was a casting director for a major television network. My experience behind the scenes led me to begin teaching acting classes as well, but my courses were unique. Rather than focusing on performance methods and concentrating on the classics, I felt it was more valuable to offer guidance in auditioning and marketing techniques. I found many talented actors were not getting the roles that would be perfect for them because they didn't know how to get their headshot and resume selected from a pile of others who, on the surface, all seemed quite similar. Then, when they did get the opportunity to audition, they didn't know how to win the role. I coached actors who were amazing on stage, but would freeze in an audition. I taught actors who had impressive resumes, but unmemorable headshots that didn't stand out from the hundreds of other candidates vying for the role. One by one I taught students how to see themselves the way a casting director would see them. I taught them to think of themselves as a product that was being sold, and showed them how to fashion themselves as merchandise that the casting director needed and were eager to buy.

This was not always a popular position to take. My students (understandably) saw themselves as individuals, not products. Some even thought this line of thinking was demeaning. Yet those who embraced this theory and worked with me to design a marketing strategy to present them to the right casting director, at the right time, with the right materials, always won out. Many of them have now gone on to enjoy tremendous career success with starring roles on popular television shows and movies. At the same time I was teaching these classes, I happened to be single. My former boss, a hugely successful casting director told me about online dating. She was enjoying multiple dates in a week and sometimes multiple dates in one day! I, too, was dating and going out to bars several times a week but after seeing my heart broken many times, she finally proclaimed that I wasn't dating "the right guys" and suggested that I try online dating. This was 2001 and online dating was still considered a little embarrassing and possibly even deviant. However, the prospect of more dates and better dates was too good for me to pass up, so I signed up for an account.

At first, I didn't even have a picture up. I was worried that someone might see me there. But after my inbox sat vacant for weeks, I realized that I needed to step up my game. Eventually, it occurred to me that my fear of being seen was unproductive. First, if someone I knew saw me online, that would mean that they were there too. Second, what was I so scared they would think seeing me? That I was single? Obviously if they knew me, they probably already knew that. My only option if I wanted to have success online was to take down my wall of insecurity and make myself not only more visible, but also more vulnerable.

I knew I had to put myself in the shoes of my students and think of myself as a product. There were thousands of men online representing thousands of opportunities for me to cast myself in my own love story. Just as I had taught the actors in my classes, it was not enough for me to know internally what I had to offer. I had to advertise myself so that they would pick me out of the online cattle call.

Yes, I saw myself as witty and attractive. But without an interesting picture and unique profile, it's no wonder I wasn't getting noticed like I knew I deserved to be. Even though I could be charming and clever with friends, I realized that if I didn't master the art of conversing with someone on a first date then I would never get past that initial phase.

So I began to approach online dating the way I was telling my actors to approach their careers. I took dating as seriously as finding a job and put time into it daily. I made my profile and pictures the best representation of the "Product Me." Eventually I met the shopper who needed that product, my future husband. He was also the very product I had been searching for.

I certainly made mistakes and there are things I would do differently if I had to do them again, but I had plenty of success. I started sharing what I'd learned with a number of friends with the hope that they could begin their online dating process that much wiser. Those friends turned into a number of clients, and those clients led me to write this book.

This dating philosophy works because it distills the process into simple ways for you to take action and change your patterns in love, just as I have for so many others already. I always tell my clients that doors will open for them. Their Mr. or Ms. Right will come along one day. But the client's job is to put in the work so they're ready when that day inevitably comes.

The right person is out there for you. Are you ready?

PART I: ONLINE
BEGIN TO SPIN

THE SYSTEM

There are two phases to spin your dating web. We'll start with Phase One: Online. This is where you learn the ins and outs of meeting someone online: How to get started, pick the best site and create a profile that will attract the right person to you. Once you have gained an understanding of how the site functions and feel that you have a profile accurately reflecting who you are and what kind of person you are looking for, you'll be ready to ease into the online dating process. You'll learn how to search effectively, send messages, set up dates and communicate comfortably online. There are also check-in questionnaires that can help you set goals and recognize your accomplishment of them.

Finding your ideal mate is usually a long-distance run rather than a sprint, so it's important to have mile markers where you can mark your progress month-by-month until you meet The One.

Once your profile starts getting noticed and you're regularly communicating with potential dates online, you'll be ready to spin Phase Two: Offline. This section guides you through the process of meeting someone for the first time face-to-face and how to make a relationship work from then on out. It also gives ideas for your first several dates, tips on meeting the parents and advice about dating in general. So even a singleton who uses only offline-dating methods could find helpful tips on how to keep a relationship going strong, plus when and how to take it to a more serious level.

Everyone takes a different length of time to achieve his or her dating goals. You may, at some point, need to back up and reevaluate your prior choices and preferences. This is not accepting failure, but rather an opportunity to know yourself that much better and to you get closer to finding someone who matches perfectly with you.

GETTING STARTED

It's important to start yourself on the right track for dating success. The more thorough you are in the beginning, the better results you'll likely have down the road. If you whiz through this process and throw a profile and picture up without much thought, your ideal mate may see it but not take you seriously. Then, even if you put the time into the process later, they still may not pay attention to your profile, having read it before and already passed you up.

I have often advised actors to do their homework before trying to get seen by casting directors. For example, if they are too anxious to get in the door and want roles they're not ready for, it's likely that a casting director will think they're too inexperienced and as a result might avoid calling them in again. But if the actors put in time to practice their craft, they're positioned to do their best work when a window of opportunity does open. There's no rush. Slow down. Take the time to get yourself set up for success.

Then proceed.

Before you begin this experience, it's really important to know what you want out of it. Do you want to get married? Do you want to become more confident at dating? Do you want to find someone special with the potential of it becoming more serious? Are you just looking to hook up?

If you're just looking to hook up, then you don't need my help. That's just as easy to find online as anything else. Just look for revealing pictures, half-baked profiles and suggestive language.

However, if you want more out of your relationships, if you're tired of chasing the wrong men or women, if you're looking to change your dating luck once and for all, then together you and I can move forward with recording your dating goals. Please begin the following worksheet.

DATING GOALS WORKSHEET

Please complete the following questions honestly:

1. I would like to meet someone to
   - ○ Date casually
   - ○ Date seriously
   - ○ Co-habitate with
   - ○ Marry
   - ○ Have children with
   - ○ (insert your goal here) _____

2. I expect this to happen in
   - ○ One month
   - ○ Three months
   - ○ Six months
   - ○ One year
   - ○ Other:_____

3. I would like to go on _____ dates in the next 3 months.

4. I would like to meet _____ different people in the next 3 months.

5. I hope dating online will
   - ○ Make me more confident in dating overall
   - ○ Introduce me to people I would not otherwise meet
   - ○ Introduce me to more serious daters
   - ○ Introduce me to a higher volume of singles
   - ○ Other:_____

SETTING GOALS

Be realistic about the time frame you place on your goals. It's unlikely that you'll meet someone you want to marry (who also wants to marry you) in the first month. It's not impossible, just unlikely.

I have, however, had clients who made a match within a few short weeks and even one who nabbed her perfect guy on her first online date ever. The potential is out there if you open yourself up to it.

This system is not magic. It cannot put your ideal mate online for you. It cannot make you more attractive. It cannot fix those personal issues you have been working for years to overcome. It cannot let you sit back and wait for him or her to materialize. But if you are committed and are willing to put in the time and effort to be successful, *Spin Your Web* can offer you more confidence, more enjoyable dating experiences and more chances to meeting your right partner online, just like many of my clients have done. Remember, you'll only get out what you put in.

For example, if you don't sign on to check your profile for many weeks, then you cannot reasonably expect to meet your goals that month. You are selling the Product You. If your best salesperson goes on sabbatical, your sales are likely to drop.

Or, if you're still on a site that you've already decided doesn't really work for you, yet you stay on because you already paid your membership fee or because you're too lazy to set up a new profile, you may not reach the right person you want to meet. You must constantly evaluate and reevaluate your dating situation, just as the owner of a startup company would check their business model to make sure they stay on track.

Learn how to track your progress and congratulate yourself for the forward movement. If you go from one date in six months to three dates in six months, that would be the kind of dating success to validate yourself for. If you get a second date when you're used to just meeting people one time and never hearing from them again, you need to give yourself credit for improving your dating patterns. Even if you don't find Mr. or Ms. Right in the first three months, you can still be able to see you are on your way and acknowledge your successful steps.

You should also continually push yourself further. Be sure that when you set new goals that you associate timelines in which to accomplish each one. If you don't reach your goal within your planned time frame, examine your actions and see what else you can do to improve yourself and your choices. If you become discouraged, look back to where you were when you first began this process and see how far you've come.

Let's take the time to record your starting point for this exciting journey in the Current Dating Snapshot.

CURRENT DATING SNAPSHOT

1. How many dates have you had in the last 6 months?

2. What is your longest relationship?

   Why do you think that came to an end?

3. Are there dating mistakes you are striving to overcome? Or is there a different type of person you hope to meet this time?

4. What do you like about your dating life now?

5. If you are new to online dating, what do you expect it to be like?

   If you are an online dating veteran, what do you hope is different about this experience?

6. What you would consider success in 3 months? 6 months? A year?

FIRST STEPS

Start by getting your head into the space of who you want to meet. Many unsuccessful daters enter the online dating realm thinking that the perfect person will somehow find them. That could be true, but if you don't know what you're truly looking for how would you even know if that person was staring you in the face? I recommend exercises to help you become better focused on what you want—or, in the case of dating, who you want. Do you always seem to pick the wrong person for you or just can't find anyone who lives up to your expectations? If so, you might want to give the following exercise a whirl:

1. Find a quiet place and think about the kind of person you want to have in your life. Imagine what he or she would look like, which qualities they would have, how they would treat you. What other aspects of your relationship are important to you? Often people say, "I don't have a type" or "I don't know what he would look like." Let's be honest, everyone—including you—has some form of an ideal love regardless of whether you ultimately end up with him or her. So this adventure is just for you. Think about who you want to meet.

2. Write down their qualities. Don't focus too much on the material or physical traits of the person. Writing down that he will be rich and handsome or that she will be a Sports Illustrated swimsuit model is not going to help you find your soul mate. Instead, focus more on the type of person. Are they generous, sweet, intellectual, artistic, detail – oriented, affectionate, ambitious or fearless? Go beyond "attractive with a good job and

sense of humor." Ninety percent of people are looking for that and, furthermore, those qualities are all relative. You may both have a sense of humor but find different things funny. Plus, they always say beauty is in the eye of the beholder. Get to the qualities that specifically appeal to your tastes and "big picture" points of view. Try to write without judgment of this person or of yourself. No one else has to see this list so you don't need to censor yourself or list a minimum or maximum number of qualities. Just write everything that is a must-have for your ideal mate.

MY IDEAL MATE

3. While you may need to return to this list if you're already with someone but are not sure they're the right one for you, for now know that by simply focusing your mind on what's important to you helps you recognize the right qualities in a mate.

4. You need to commit to at least three months to this process. Check your account three or more times per week. Always be proactive about sending out emails, regardless of your views on proper gender roles. Sometimes my female clients have a hard time embracing this because they feel it's important to be courted. I prefer to look at the online portion of this process as dating strategy rather than actual dating. When you understand the backend operation of an online dating site, it makes it a concept rather than an action and therefore easier to grasp.

How it works: Most sites rank your matches based upon complex algorithms. The same way that Google knows how to present the ads to you that they think you're more likely to click on, online dating sites send you matches they think would appeal to you based on your prior behavior on the site. Think of how many times Google has sent you an advertisement that wasn't actually right for you. However, on a site like Groupon where you have a list of deals to choose from, you may be more likely to find a product you connect with because you are searching through the vendors yourself.

Online dating works in a similar way. Algorithms may be keeping you from someone that strikes your fancy for a variety of computer-generated reasons. Therefore, if you see someoene you want to talk to, you should take the first step to reach out to them. Do not assume that they'll reach out to you because you may not be coming up in their searches. They also may be inactive on the site but reading your message might entice them to come back online. These are just some of the reasons you need to set aside your ideas about who makes the first online move. The courtship really begins on that initial date.

Also note that winks, pokes and other notifications that don't include a personal message do not count. If you don't actually compose something specifically tailored for someone, it'll seem like you aren't serious. I once had a very attractive and accomplished client who told me in our first session that he preferred to send out a form letter for his initial communication. He would send 10 to 20 letters a week, but only receive one or two responses back. So only to those one or two would he begin to compose individual replies. He felt that he had such a low rate of response that it didn't matter what he said in that first email and he didn't want to waste time writing distinct messages for each woman since he assumed that no matter what he wrote, he'd get the same level of interest.

Where I felt he was going wrong was in the first step of sending a very obvious form letter. Even though he had a lot going for him when you read his profile, his initial contact with a woman came in a way that made her feel like a number rather than as someone special to whom he was uniquely attracted.

My first exercise taught him how to craft personalized emails that would express what interested him in the intended recipient worded in a way that would not be overwhelmingly time consuming.

The basic format is similar to what you learned about writing a cover letter for a resume submission:

ɔentence 1: What Caught Your Eye.

In this sentence you tell the person why they stood out to you. The more obsure the reference that you comment on or the more knowledgeable you seem about their job, hometown or favorite activities, the better your chances at getting their attention.

EXAMPLE: "I love that you're also a huge fan of Stephen King. His stories can really keep me awake all night. My favorite is still IT."

Sentence 2: What They Should Notice About You.

This is your time to shine. Highlight something that they will find interesting to learn in your profile. Be careful that this does not just turn into a bragging moment. Position your statement based on how it relates to them and what they've said in their profile.

EXAMPLE: "I talk all about my irrational fear of clowns in my profile. And snakes. And cruise ships."

Sentence 3: Imagine Yourselves Together.

In the closing sentence you should write something that evokes a picture of you in their life or, more simply, a suggestion of something you could do together.

EXAMPLE: "Maybe we can go for a stroll in a pet cemetary sometime, seems a lot safer to me than the boardwalk with all those sideshows and ports."

You need to actively seek out potential dates and send emails on a regular basis. I'm speaking to both sexes here. You must think of this part of the courtship as more strategic planning than actual dating. If you think of every message that you don't get a response from as rejection, you'll burn out quickly. There are a variety of reasons why someone might not be responding to you. They could've just begun a relationship, they could have a very narrow idea of what they're looking for and it doesn't quite line up with you, or this could be a fake or inactive profile. You cannot online date successfully with thin skin. Picture each message as a coin dropped in a fountain. If your wish comes true—wonderful, but you probably aren't put out much by losing a penny if it doesn't. And, you certainly aren't thinking about that wish weeks later or telling yourself that you will never throw a coin in a fountain again.

Even if you don't get responses immediately, keep at it. The more you send, the better you will get at composing messages and the easier the words will come to you. Remember, it only takes one perfect match to make it all worthwhile!

The Product "You"

The biggest obstacle to successful online dating is that most people have no idea how to advertise who they are or who they are looking for. So from this point forward, I want you to think of yourself as a product: The Product "You." You've been in beta testing for this product your entire life. Now it's time to release the premium model into the marketplace. The goal is to sell as many units of this product until you feel rich and secure enough to not need to sell it anymore.

Let's look at your marketing plan. How do you wish to be perceived by dates? It's important that when you have a product to sell you know why a potential buyer would look at it and say "I want that!" It's equally as important to know everything about the product you're selling and be realistic about its functionality. If you're selling a Toyota, your marketing campaign needs to be about reliability. Whereas if you're selling a Ferrari, your message is about speed. If you try to present your Toyota as a flashy, slick, speed demon, you'll have a lot of disappointed buyers—or worse, a lot of cars left on your lot. But if you realize your Toyota's greatest asset is its reliability and you successfully highlight all the related benefits—like less money spent on repairs and better gas mileage—then you target your advertisement to buyers who need just that. Your Toyotas can be in high demand amongst the right audience. Sure, a Ferrari is a flashier car, but how many people can afford them or truly want them when they realize what they actually need?

Yes, there are physically perfect "10s" in the dating world. But what's behind someone's good looks? A shiny new car loses 20 percent of its value the moment it's driven off the lot. So the most physically attractive daters may get the most activity initially, but that doesn't mean they're the most likely to meet their right match and sustain a long-term relationship.

Starting to see the parallels but still unsure of what your product is? The "Product Me" Marketing worksheet below can serve as a reminder that it's okay to be yourself online and offline.

If you get nervous on first dates, try referring to your list of positive qualities to boost your confidence. The more confident you are and the more you can allow your true self to shine through, the more likely you are to attract a mate who is looking for someone just like you.

PRODUCT YOU DISTRIBUTION: THE WEB

Choosing the right dating website is as important as choosing the right store. You could buy a book at the pharmacy, but you would have a larger selection at a better price if you went to Barnes & Noble or Amazon. In the same way you determine the kind of product you are, think about which store would be best for the buyers you want. You wouldn't go to Home Depot if you want to buy groceries. So if you're looking for a serious relationship, you likely won't find it on a swingers' site. There are many factors in selecting a site that is best suited for you, but when you put yourself in the mindset of selling a product, it's easier to define where you'll reach the "buyers" who are most likely to be interested in the product of YOU.

"PRODUCT YOU" MARKETING WORKSHEET

1. What are your best qualities; the ones you openly share when you are comfortable with someone?

2. What qualities do you present on a first date?

3. Are there qualities you desire to show more?

4. What would you want someone to say about you after the date?

5. What are your weaker qualities?
   What are you working to improve on?

6. What would you liken your "Product YOU" to?

7. What do you find most appealing about this product?

8. What kind of person do you think would be attracted to this product?

BUILD YOUR WEB

The Right Site

Currently, most sites operate on a "pay to communicate" model. This means you can join the site, create a profile and search through their members at no charge. This classification of membership may only give access to certain featured profiles, but it will give you some understanding of the kind of clients that site attracts.

Most traditional dating sites offer a fee-based monthly membership, while others work on a credit system where you pay per message. There are also free sites that are generally ad-supported. There's nothing wrong with these free sites, but keep in mind that the more someone spends for a dating service, the more serious they're likely to be. And if $0 is what they're willing to spend, it raises questions about how invested they are in meeting someone special.

How to Evaluate a Site

1. Are there people on the site you are attracted to?
2. Do the other daters seem to be compatible with you? Do they enjoy the same activities? Are they from a comparable culture? Do they practice the same religion? Do they share similar political views? Do they come from an equivalent socio-economic background? The questions to ask are based

on what is important to you. Studies have shown that similar values are a greater predictor of longevity in a relationship than similar interests.

3. Do you like the functionality and navigation of the site? Do you see yourself using video? If not, maybe that is something you don't want to pay for. Do you like to instant message? If so, does the site offer that feature? How many pictures does the site allow you to display? Can you write your own answers or do you have to pick them from a multiple choice field? Do you find it easy to search and review results?

What Kind of Pool Do You Want to Swim In?

Several large sites attract a very wide pool of potential mates. This means your volume of dates is likely to be higher, but you may have to work harder to find those who you are most compatible with or who share your interests.

If you go with a more specialized pool, you likely will have fewer dates due to there being fewer members who match your criteria. However, though there are fewer options, you're likely to have more in common with those in the pool. You might also run into people you know if you already spend time with singles in that social circle.

Dating Site Options

Mass Market Sites (Example: Match.com)

Lots of people. Lots of options. Lots of work. They have the greatest selection and some of the most varied features and competitive pricing, but what you have to be ready for is the volume. You have to be willing to put real time in to find those you have the most in common with. For those of you who like to do things on your terms and make your own decisions, this is the type of site for you.

Compatability-Based Sites (Example: eHarmony.com)

This kind of site is good for someone without much time to devote to searching or who likes to have a guiding hand in making selections. eHarmony has what they call a "scientifically-based" matching system where they suggest matches for you. It does not allow for open searching the way that Match.com does. Instead, the site offers you a list of matches based upon your answers to an extensive personality questionnaire. Then it steers communication between you and a potential partner, offering you a select group of multiple-choice questions and answers which the two of you exchange. Conversation is controlled by the site until you progress through a series of levels and pass the "guided communication" phase. If you prefer however, you can fast-track communication and select your own questions, so there is flexibility in case you prefer more structure. eHarmony tends to attract daters looking for a serious relationship because of the time committment needed just to complete the personality survey. It's also one of the most expensive online dating sites.

Free Sites (Example: PlentyofFish.com)

POF is a free service that's one of the most popular sites in the United States, United Kingdom and Canada. It gets a lot of hits, but many are from casual daters who are not interested in a long-term relationship, either wanting to hook up or entertain themselves by chatting online. Yet, if you know that many of those you meet there may not be looking to settle down any time soon, then you certainly still can connect with a lot of potential dates.

Niche Sites (Example: JDate.com)

If cultural background or religion is a deal-breaker to you, then I suggest you go directly to a site that specializes in your desired group. However, not everyone on these sites is of that particular identification. If you aren't from that background but are interested in dating someone who is, you may find that you like in this more targeted pool that they may be there looking for someone of that specific group so don't take it personally if you don't get the volume of responses you normally would on other sites. A niche site can also represent a particular interest or activity, so if finding someone who will go on yoga retreats or run with you is very important, consider signing up for a site that's focused around those interests. However, the more narrow the category, the more sparse the pool generally is, therefore you may have to open yourself up to dating ouside of your immediate geographic area if you're set on using a niche site.

Social-Dating Sites (Example: HowAboutWe.com)

As social networking becomes a bigger part of our lives, dating sites are turning more of their attention towards creating an online dating community with more interaction between daters online or using your existing social network to procure more dates. Some sites are simply using your own interests to generate date ideas and create communities around certain activities within a larger dating site. Others tap into your Facebook or Twitter account to help you meet people that are within a few degrees of separation from you or introduced directly by your social-networking friends.

Check out two or three sites and use the worksheet that follows to compare and contrast which is best for you. If it's affordable for you, I would recommend posting a profile on more than one site. You may notice a difference in both how you are perceived and how many people you connect with between the various sites. Using two dating sites allows you to be in two places at the same time, thereby doubling your chances for success. Usually I do not suggest that my clients use more than two sites at a time because it can become difficult to keep up with messages and stay active on multiple sites. On most sites, one predictor of how visible you are when someone conducts a search is the amount of time you spend actively using the site. So make sure you're checking in and conducting searches frequently to get the most bang for your buck and highest frequency of profile views.

DATING GOALS WORKSHEET

	Site #1 Name	Site #2 Name	Site #3 Name
Selection & Quality of Daters			
Positives of Functionality			
Negatives of Functionality			
I Wish This Site Had or Did...			
Site Cost Per Month/Value for Function			
Rate of Response to Emails Sent			

The Right Screen Name

Choosing your user name is as important as naming and branding a product. Pick a name that represents who you are and the kind of person you are looking to meet. Avoid using your actual name unless you combine it with a descriptive quality. Also avoid using arbitrary numbers. If you want to use numbers, then make them relevant to who you are or who you want to meet. Your screen name can be one that will make more sense as someone gets to know you. However don't choose one so obscure that nobody will be intrigued enough to click on it in the first place. I recommend choosing an actual word rather than initials or letters. That way you'll be more memorable. Below are some examples:

Joseph714—Maybe 714 is the area code for where Joseph grew up in. Or maybe Joseph lives within the 714 area code and is searching in that vicinity. Or maybe those numbers relate to his birthday or that of a family member. There are many intriguing possibilities that come to mind when you see this name. However, if 714 has no real relevance to his life then it's a missed opportunity to tell a potential date something about himself.

SexKittenAH—Let's say Ashley or AH wants to be in a serious relationship but she names herself this thinking it will better attract a man because, well, sex sells. She's right. Sex will sell her just that...sex. If she wants a guy to take her seriously and if she wants to meet a guy who's serious in return, then she would be better off choosing a name that conveys other information about her. Perhaps she is always complimented on her eyes. If so, she could turn heads with screen name AshleyBabyBlue.

AviatorJoe tells more than just Joe32936. Joe likes to fly so that means he's adventurous. You can also deduce that he is dedicated to and invested in being a pilot. Most aviators are also well traveled. There's a lot you can discover from that short screen name.

TennisProLen gives you an immediate sense that this guy is active, likes the outdoors and is competitive in nature. Len is more likely to get clicked on just because his screen name is informative. Plus, confidence is sexy. While some people might find it obnoxious that Len put Pro in his name, more will likely find it intriguing.

Even the way you write your name says a lot about who you are. *Mikey2323* is someone who you'd expect to be playful and youthful while variations like *MNP2323* or even *Mike2323* come off as more generic.

Perhaps there's a pun or something catchy you can play with in your name. Maybe Ramon could be *EvrybdyXORamon*. But don't get too clever with abbreviations. If someone cannot understand what your profile means, they will never click on it. For example, *LookN4the1* could easily be misread and it takes too long to get at first glance. Plus names that talk about your interest in finding love usually read as cheesy or insincere and don't say anything unique about you.

You do not need to use your real name at all. In fact, the more interesting names usually relate to qualities or interests instead, which holds much more value in a relationship than just a name. Remember that you are selling 'The Product You' and this is the first point of contact that a potential date would have with your brand.

If you find a name that works, stick with it. When some people join second or third sites, they feel the need to reinvent themselves each time. If someone has already reviewed your profile on another site and made a decision about you, then seeing the same specific name will cut to the chase for both of you even if you're on a different site. Lastly, if a Product You changes their name, how would you ever know how to find it again?

THE RIGHT PIC

A picture makes you want to take a closer look at a product online. Yet, understandably, often new online daters are skittish about posting their picture. I think about it this way: Would you pick out a shirt online without seeing what it looks like? Or, what if you had the option of buying two shirts at the same price and one had a photo and the other didn't? How could you expect potential dates to click on your profile if you don't have a picture? Being online is a visual experience so you have to set aside the fear that someone you know might see you and just put yourself out there.

Don't you hate it when you see something online, say a hotel room, and book it, but when you arrive you find the room's actually smaller that it seemed online, the carpet is dirty and the amenities all need to be serviced? This strategy may work for the hotel for a while. Eventually though, angry guests will start to retaliate and, by word of mouth, the truth will get around. This will cause the chances of repeat customers to become severly limited and the business will not likely be able to sustain itself. This applies to online photos and is why you need to skip the glamour shots. Forget the picture you took five years ago that you always thought you looked hot in. Forget the one when you had lost ten pounds before shortly gaining back fifteen. The most important quality for your picture is that it looks like the current you. Your profile should feature three to five photos—more than that and you may be giving away too much., less than that and it might seem like you have something to hide. The goal is to meet online as a way to then meet in person. Give them just enough to be intrigued and nothing to turn them away too soon.

THE MUST-HAVE PICS

1. The Everyday You. This is to be a representation of you at your best. But most importantly, it must actually look like you. What most folks don't realize is that you probably already have this picture. Maybe it was taken when you were out with some friends having a good time. Or maybe it was a picture your mom took of you relaxing on a holiday. This picture should seem effortless, you don't want to come off as trying too hard, and should accurately reflect the qualities you mention in your profile. Also make sure that your face can be clearly seen. No sunglasses or wacky accessories that sell you as someone different than the person who will arrive on that first date.

2. The Other Side of You. If you are generally energetic, this photo is to be of the more subdued you. If you are quiet and reserved, this is the picture that shows you let go every once in a while. Wearing bold accessories in this picture is fine as long as you have a clear representation of who you really are in your "Everyday You" photo.

3. The Activity Picture. This photo showcases what you like to do and what's important to you. If you enjoy hiking and the outdoors then use a picture from a recent outing. If you like to play a particular sport then post a picture of you in the height of the moment. This could be your artsy, world traveler photo. Or that wild picture of you skydiving.

Other pictures can be any variation of your personality and lifestyle. But there are a few things to keep in mind:

- You should be the star of your primary picture. No other people, eye-catching backgrounds or things that obscure your lovely face. Anything that can detract attention from you does not belong in your "Everyday You" shot.
- Edit your pics. Changing little things like the height and width ratio of the photo, how much skin you show or distance from your head to the edge of the picture can make a huge difference. Be sure to properly showcase what you want people to notice, such as your smile or your eyes. This is not a license to go photo-editing crazy and modify things about your appearance. Adjusting the exposure is different than using a slimming effect or changing your eye color, and it's important to stay on the side of reality when you begin tweaking pictures.
- Avoid photos with other people or with people blatantly cropped out. Even if on a subconscious level, a potential suitor may see that phantom arm around you and wonder who it belongs to. If it's possible to cleanly edit the photo, however, I'm all for using it. I worked with someone who posted a picture of himself with his nephew as his primary

photo. His goal was to show that he was a guy who loved his family and kids. However, the message that photograph sent was, "Here's my son. If you don't accept him then don't even bother." It was clear in the written portion of his profile that he had no children. But I'm sure a number of women saw that picture and didn't read further. As soon as he switched out that photo though, he met the woman who is now his wife and have two beautiful children of their own.

- Stay away from drinking or drunk pictures. Some people like to send the message, "I'm a fun, party girl/guy." That's fine if you aren't looking for anything serious. But if you are, then you don't need to show that side of you now. They can read about it in your profile and see how much fun you are when you actually meet. Otherwise, you risk turning off a number of great dates before they even meet you.

- Don't just take a picture with your webcam. It will look hasty and overtly casual. There's really no excuse for not having a good digital photo of yourself with the technology now available at our fingertips. Choosing a picture that says something is much smarter than just throwing up a picture for the sake of having something there.

- Avoid taking photos of yourself in a mirror. Not only do some daters find it creepy, but it can make people think that you're a loner without anyone else to take a picture of you. Remember that you can repurpose pictures from any event or outing. You don't necessarily need to take a photo specifically for a dating site. So, unless you really are that much of an outcast or you're extremely camera-shy, there must be some photo others have taken of you that you could use.

- Make sure you have a mix of face and body shots. Remember you have to abide by the rule of truth-in-advertising. So if you only have face shots, it may seem like you're hiding something.

- No nude pictures or even excessively revealing ones— unless your goal is a one-night stand, because that's the message you'll be sending. I had a client who wanted to use a photo of her in a low-cut top because she thought it would get her more messages. It's true that it might, but I questioned whether or not she would get messages from the kind of men she wanted to date, guys who were interested in a long-term relationship. Since one-night stands did not line up with her dating goals, she decided against using the picture and ultimately felt better about not objectifying herself.

Spin Your Profile

Your profile is probably the most important part of selling the Product You. Your picture can draw someone to click on you, but if you don't have a profile that comes up in a search and captures someone's interest once they get beyond your picture, then you won't stand out from the thousands of other daters who, on the surface, seem very similar to you.

The Right Tag Line

The tagline (or headline) always seems to produce the most

anxiety amongst my clients. Do not overthink this. For example, you can pick a quote from a movie you love. Or a phrase your mom always said to you. Maybe something you always joke about with your best friend. It could be a little obscure or uninteresting to the wrong person, but direct and amusing to the right one. Avoid anything sexually suggestive since that won't attract anyone who's interested in a serious, long-term relationship. Actually short and sweet is preferable. Some sites now use your answer to a specific question as your headline. HowAboutWe.com for example, prompts you to suggest a date activity and that then becomes the text associated with your picture in search results.

LONG-FORM RESPONSES

In your written profile responses, the most important thing is honesty. You need to be the person that you describe yourself as when you meet face-to-face. The second most important factor in making your profile stand out is specificity. Rather than simply listing what you like to do, tell a compelling story that demonstrates your point. Be brief but effective. In this first interaction, people don't want to read a novel about you, but they do need to have enough detail that they can paint a picture about who you are in their mind.

On occasion, I've had clients say that they had a friend write their profile for them. Sometimes I have been asked to craft clients' profiles on their behalf. In my opinion, this sells your profile short. I can make suggestions about how to phrase what you're trying to say in a more charming, comedic or direct way. I can tease a great story out of you to bring your profile to life. But overall, the most important info that you want to communicate to a potential partner can only be created by you. If you cannot make the time to construct your own profile, do you really have the time to devote to a relationship? If you cannot sing your own praises or find interesting stories to tell about your life when you have ample time to compose your answers, how will you interest someone when you're on a date? If you're nervous about your writing ability, there are many professionals like myself who can help you express yourself more effectively, but you have to start somewhere. Go back to your list of who you want to attract. Now visualize yourself answering the questions in your profile in person to that man or woman.

One mistake I see daters make is talking about what they don't want in a mate rather than what they do want. When things are not working, it's easy to point to what's not pleasing you about your current dating situation. Or to say, "I know I don't want that" when referring to your last relationship. Nobody wants to meet someone who feels inferior or broken in some way. So rather than focusing on the negative, use your profile to showcase what you love about yourself and advertise to the person who would best complement those qualities.

SAY WHAT YOU WANT

Don't be embarrassed to say exactly what you want here. Trying to sound too cool won't catch anyone's attention. Saying something like, "I'm just looking for an easy-going girl to hang out with" reads that you're just looking to fool around. If that's what you're after, by all means put it out there so no one gets the wrong impression. But if you want to meet your soul mate and settle down, don't tap dance around it. This is the place to be direct and focused on meeting the right person.

SELECTING SHORT-FORM RESPONSES

The biggest mistake I see is when people don't want to turn off anyone and will essentially select every option in a short-answer question. That says nothing about you. Try to be selective about the answers that really matter to you. Choosing everything is as informative as choosing nothing at all.

DATE LIKE IT'S YOUR JOB

One of the basics of the online dating experience is building a habit to regularly and effectively communicate online. It can be nerve-wracking to do so, but it can also be one of the most exciting parts of the process.

If you're new to online dating, promise yourself that you'll send at least five messages a week for the first month. Then each month add at least one more message per week. Make it your goal to turn at least two messages per month into a phone call and one of those phone calls into a date.

For a more seasoned dater, go back to your prior messages and read them again after completing this guide. Evaluate where you may have not been servicing the Product You as well as you could, and try again.

Wherever you are, make sure you're regularly taking stock of your progress. It's easy to get frustrated if you have not met your ideal mate in a month, but if you see that you're going on more dates and putting more effort into meeting the right person, you're giving yourself a better chance at success.

I say to my most motivated clients, "You need to date like it's your job." Only when you're putting out maximum effort can you expect maximum results.

THE RULES FOR ONLINE COMMUNICATION

SEARCH CRITERIA

First you must find someone you want to write to. As a general rule you want to take your ideal search criteria and automatically expand it by one or two options. If you want to meet a guy who is six feet tall, et your criteria for 5'8" to 6'4". If you'd really prefer to meet someone within 10 miles of you, stretch yourself to 25 miles. If you're constantly seeking only Mr. or Ms. Exactly Perfectly-Right, you'll definitely be frustrated by your results. With the automatic search you could be ruling out the person of your dreams who happens to be just an inch shorter, a pound heavier or brown-eyed instead of blue.

I got lucky in meeting my husband, but I could've easily missed him. I was 24 and was seeking an older man, so I searched only 25 and up. Little did I know when I signed up for this site, that the man who fit every single quality I was looking for wasn't going to be 25 for another two months. Had he not written to me, I may have signed off before finding him, or before he turned 25.

START WITH A POINT OF REFERENCE

It's always impressive to know that someone actually reads

the words you painstakingly compose in your profile. That's why you should be sure to refer to something specific in their profile when you email a potential date. Find something you agree with, disagree on, or have a thought about and make a comment on it followed by asking a question. Sincere questions beg for answers so you're better positioned to get a response if you ask something specific to what they've written rather than a generic note that just tells them they caught your eye.

NO WINKS!

Winks and virtual gifts are pointless. They merely say, "I think your picture is cute, but I can't think of anything clever to say." Maybe you spent $10 to send a bouquet of virtual roses, but what message does that send? "I couldn't take the time to write something but I can buy your affections." If you're really serious about reaching out to someone, writing a personal note will take you further.

ASK AND YE SHALL RECEIVE

Be proactive and send messages frequently. Maybe he's not your perfect type but he has the funniest profile you've ever read. Perhaps she lives a little further than you want to travel for a date but she's perfect in every other way. Just put it out there. And don't judge it. If you don't get a response, just move on to the next. There are so many fish in the cybersea it's not worth over-thinking it. Women, do not be afraid to send messages. Men, do not let your ego get bruised if you have to send more messages than you originally thought. Bolster yourself by knowing it only takes the right one to make all the effort worthwhile.

The Rule of Three
Part A

Have no more than three exchanges online before moving to a phone call. There are definitely people online who have no intention of meeting anyone in person. You can weed out the ones who are wasting your time pretty quickly. Some sites have been criticized for posting fake profiles and even using internal employees to communicate with daters to keep you on the site. The bigger reason why this rule is important to you is that the longer you stay online, the more you will tend to create a mental portrait of the person on the other end.

If they end up not being who you thought they were once you meet them, you'll generally end up disappointed and it'll be impossible for that person to morph into who you want them to be. If you want to buy a house, you wouldn't commit to a mortgage after only seeing a few pictures and talking to the realtor for a few months. You'd go see the property and determine if it's still your dream home when you view it first-hand.

Try the Instant Messenger

An IM session counts as one online exchange. It can give a lot of information about a person's sense of humor, conversation skills and temperament without the stress of a face-to-face date. You should move to a phone call after an IM session though to keep the communication moving forward.

Face-to-Face
Trumps Cyberconversation

After the first successful phone call you must make a plan for a date. I sugggest that if you're still interested at that point, make a move to set the first date by the end of the call. Generally, if you don't want to meet the person face-to-face after talking to them by phone, it's not going to be better in person. If a mention of meeting up is not made in this call, then it means at least one of you isn't really into the other.

Short and Sweet

Keep the first call to 30 minutes or less. Don't show your hand to soon. You want the call to be a teaser. Get a sense that the other person is not a psycho, an incessant talker or a bigot. If they're not, meet them face-to-face.

You want to have something to discuss in person in spite of the first date jitters. The multiple phone conversation pattern has the same effect as the multiple email pattern. You create an idea of a person who doesn't exist. The rule of thumb is to meet in person as soon as possible.

To Text or Not to Text

Texting has a rightful place in relationship communication but it's best used only to share short details. That's why there's a character limit. Communicating only through text will make you seem juvenile and afraid of direct interaction. One of my clients shared that she almost turned down a date invitation from a man with whom she ended up in a long-term relationship because he asked her out over text. Not only does it make your date feel unimportant to you, but you can also risk communications being misinterpreted when they come in short snippets rather than in spoken words.

Skype Dating

My rule on virtual dating used to be a hard and fast NO. However, when one of my clients met a man that she fell madly in love with on eHarmony.com who lived on the other side of the country, I had to change my tune. Since they could not initially meet in person, their next best option was Skype dating. But, rather than just sitting at their computers in their sweatpants, they made real dates out of it. They would schedule a sushi date and both pick up their favorite rolls, then meet online to share a meal together. Once they found out that they had a connection on video, they flew to meet one another and it happened to work out. If your only option to see your date is via video chat, make sure you are approaching it as an actual date. You don't get a second chance to make a first impression.

The Rules for the First Date

Always Meet Them There

No matter how long you talked to this person online, how many nights you've stayed up talking to them on the phone, or how close you live to one another, you do not know them yet. A) Better to be safe than sorry and B) Feeling trapped is never good.

Meet for Drinks

Coffee, wine or beer? It doesn't matter. But your first date should always be a mini – one, or at least start out that way. Give yourself a chance to have that awkward "now we can see what one another actually looks like" moment without feeling like you have to stay through dessert if things don't go smoothly. If things do go well, then you have the option of ordering more, but there's no pressure if it's just drinks.

Stick to One Location

Even if you hit it off right away, it's a good idea to space out your dates. If you want to keep talking, see if you can sustain that through the second and third dates. Don't wear yourself weary with another date just after the first one the night before.

Set a Cutoff Limit

My cutoff limit was always one drink, which I had to figure out the hard way. The one time since when I last exceeded that limit, was the night I met my husband. Your tolerance may be higher than mine, but set a number that will keep you from getting lax on the rules, or worse yet, forgetting the rules altogether. Your cutoff limit may also be a time limit. Say 90 minutes. It's always good to be coming from somewhere and going somewhere after. That lets them know they aren't the only game in town for you and gives you a pre-determined exit strategy should you need it. Even if it's going well it's better to leave them wanting more and end on a high note.

Trust Your Gut

If you get a strange feeling about someone, trust yourself. I had a friend who let a guy pick her up on the first date and he ended up nearly starting a fistfight at the bar with a fellow he thought was hitting on her. So they went to another location where things only got uglier. She kept wanting to give him the benefit of the doubt, but it ended up being a total waste of her time. She could have saved three hours of her life if she pulled the plug on the date when he first got heated. In spite of these online dating faux pas, things could have gone very dfferently with a guy that volatile. Thank God she's happily married with a child now.

You can't let one mistake dictate another. You must always be in control. She made the mistake of letting him pick her up, but she did not need to return with him. It would be well-worth the cab fare to get away from a guy like that. Meeting in a public place ensures that there will be others to help you avoid a bad situation. For example, a restaurant will always call you a cab if you request one. And you do not need to go to your place. Instead, find a friend with a secure home or apartment and go there if you think your date may surface later. If things get really bad, just drive straight to the nearest police department. If the date from hell has dark intentions, they won't follow you there.

I don't say these things to scare you, I say them to make you aware and to encourage you to pay attention to what you're feeling. Online dating is just as safe as meeting a potential date through any other avenue. But, with any instance of meeting someone new, exercise caution and listen to your intuition until you get to know one another better.

Rule of Three, Part B

So many times I hear, "Well, I wasn't attracted to him right away. He didn't look like his picture." Hate to tell you, but there's more to meeting your mate than instant attraction. All you need to know by the end of the first date is if they are interesting enough for you to want to hear more of their story. All you need to know by the end of the second date is that your attention is captured enough to want to spend a third date with them. If you feel no sparks by the end of the third date you're probably better off as friends, but at least you have given true love a shot.

Of course there are people who seem to know they have something special the first time they meet. But, more often than not, it's not like that and you should avoid judging or trying to put a label on your thoughts and feelings until you've reached the third date. However, if there's no physical or mental attraction after date one; if the other person doesn't make you smile or laugh, there's no need to be a martyr by trying to make it work.

NEXT DATE

If you think this person is interesting, it's absolutely okay to propose a second date regardless of your gender. At the very least you should promise a future phone call. Newsflash gentlemen: Calling a girl three, six or nine days later doesn't send the message that you're slick, cool or have got it goin' on. It sends the message that you aren't that interested. Guess what happens when a girl becomes disinterested in you? Game over. She may give you another shot, but then you're already working uphill to win her back. You'd probably be better off starting over with someone else. And women, don't play too hard to get. When a guy is ready to find a relationship, he will tire very quickly of games. So if you like him, don't play games. If a man gets the sense that you aren't interested in him, even if he likes you, he'll sometimes avoid calling you in an effort to protect himself from rejection. Bottom line, if you're interested in someone, do not be afraid to show it.

Part II: Offline
CATCH YOUR PREY

WELCOME BACK

Congratulations. If you've moved on to Part Two it means you've navigated the strange and wonderful process of connecting with someone online. But building a cyber-relationship is only half the battle. Your ultimate goal is to meet someone with whom you can build a relationship—and maybe even a life with—in the real world. This is where you begin to take the greatest risks and reap the greatest rewards.

By now you may have seen at least a couple of people and found at least one person who you want to get to know better. It's acceptable in this phase (and even encouraged) for you to date multiple people while you figure things out. When you make a big purchase like a car, you don't just buy the first one you see. You test drive. You go to different dealers to find the perfect color and model. And, you negotiate a deal. Online dating is much the same.

As long as you are upfront and honest, no one can fault you for enjoying yourself and making the most of your dating-site membership fees. This's also the time when it's okay to make dating mistakes, as long as you learn from them and do not repeat them.

Or perhaps you've found someone you really like and you're saying to yourself, "I've gotten this far, how do I keep myself from screwing it up?" Here's something to keep in mind: Someone is either going to be the right one for you, or they aren't. People often beat themselves up about what they said wrong or should've said, but couldn't find the courage to get it out. Release yourself from that kind of thinking and know that your right mate won't be keeping a scorecard for you. If it's meant to be, and you follow the guidelines below, it will happen for you. If it's not meant to ne, you will still have the tools to get back in the game and try again.

LeBron James didn't sink his first freethrow, and probably not his third or fourth either. But the more he played, the easier the game became for him, just as the dating game will become easier for you.

The Rules for Offline Communication
Eight Date Outline

All relationships progress at various speeds. If it feels right and you sense that your partner is on the same page, there is no right or wrong length of time. However, I've outlined the ideal scenario for eight dates, which is generally the point where things get serious or fizzle out.

Date One

I cannot stress this strongly enough: Just do drinks. This should only be an hour to an hour-and-a-half meeting. Remember to always be arriving from somewhere and leaving to another place. I had dates that lasted as little as 30 minutes, and let me tell you, we were both glad that we didn't have to spend another half-hour waiting for the veal to arrive.

Date Two

Don't go overboard. It's still not time for a steak dinner. You're getting to know one another. This date allows you an opportunity to showcase something you enjoy. For example, your favorite restaurant or pub. Or an activity you could pair with conversation like pool, arcade games or miniature golf. Bowling is not recommended as one of you is always sitting while the other is bowling, making it a better group activity than date. If you really want to impress them, try something unique that lets your date know you're tapped into your local scene.

Date Three

This date is the decision-maker of the first phase of dating. Now is the time to lay it on a little thicker. Go for the famous chef's bistro or the hard-to-get-a-reservation spot. You're far enough in to go to a movie now. As long as conversation is included before and after, you should be comfortable to sit in the dark without speaking at this point. My husband and I went to a concert on this date. Not only was it romantic to hear music with him, but we had an hour car ride in each direction so by the time I got back I felt like I knew the real him.

Date Four

This is a good daytime date. That's when you really get to know someone. In the light of day people become who they truly are. Go for a hike and then grab lunch. Attend an amusement park or fair. See a baseball game. Go sailing. Play tennis or golf together—make sure the other person is truly into the sport and isn't just going along with you. Playing a game with someone can tell you a lot about who they are.

Date Five

By now you should be over the major jitters. You should know one another well enough to experience each other's world first-hand. Perhaps a movie at someone's house? Cooking dinner for one another—or better yet, together. But keep it simple. My husband tried to make pasta from scratch the first time he cooked for me. Though the meal was essentially inedible, I fortunately found it unbelievably flattering that he would go to such lengths to impress me. You probably will feel better in the end, however, if you cook something that you know you'll be successful at.

Date Six

The fancy date. If you have the means, this would be a good time to take in a special activity. That doesn't necessarily mean expensive, just one where you dress up in more than jeans. For example, many museums have special events a couple of evenings a month. Or see live theatre. Take in a concert. Whatever it is, make sure you discuss with your date what you're interested in doing so that you can see if it's something they would like as well. And for the invitee, just because it's something you've never done before, don't say no. A right partner will expand your horizons and show you new things.

Date Seven

The person you are dating shouldn't be asked to spend time with your friends or family until at least this point. Make sure they like you before making sure they like your friends. A lot of people make the mistake of bringing along a wingman for the first couple of dates to make sure it's a good fit. The trouble with that is the date will rarely feel comfortable enough to open up to you and your buddy at the same time. It's a lot harder for the sparks to fly when you have someone blocking or absorbing them.

Date Eight

Assuming you two are going out together once or twice a week, this would be an appropriate time to suggest a day trip. A change of locale could help keep things interesting. Maybe a day of skiing, wine tasting or a trip to the beach. Anything that will keep you both intrigued with each other. But don't belabor it with pressure to stay overnight.

GENERAL RULES

• All dates should not only be suggested by one person in the couple all of the time.

• Activities should be discussed and agreed upon by both of you until you know one another well enough. Then you might want to surprise the other with something you know they'll like.

• In the beginning, I'd advise seeing each other no more than twice a week. A lot of people get so excited when they find a new friend that they jump in without looking where they are going. Pacing yourself will keep you interested longer and build more excitement for each meeting, fending off the tendency to take one another for granted.

THE MOST MAJOR RULE OF THEM ALL

You might hate me for saying this, and you may not see the point until later down the road, but if you're looking for a serious relationship, I recommend not having sex until at least date five. You want to truly get to know someone, so give yourself a chance to become acquainted without the confusion of sex. I've never heard someone say, "I wish I didn't wait so long". It's always the opposite. A lot of people rush into the physical part of a relationship and that begins to color their perception of what's actually going on. Sometimes this confusion leads to staying in a bad situation for months longer than you should.

I'm not saying no physical intimacy at all. I'm only saying sex will be that much more rewarding the longer you allow the tension to build and become more familiar and comfortable with your partner. If you're serious about someone, you will want to invest the time in getting to know them. And if they're anxious to get things cooking sooner, that could be a red flag about their intentions with online dating.

Some of you may feel nervous about sounding like a prude when turning down sex before the fifth date. Here are some suggestions for how you can frame it:

"I feel like we're connecting and I think that having sex now could keep me from really getting to know you."

"I've had experiences in the past when I got physical before I was ready and it ended up messing things up. I really like you and I don't want that to happen here."

"I want our first time to be really special and memorable. I think it'll be better if we wait until we know each other better."

"I'm following some advice to wait until at least date five. This friend's been right so far, so I'm going to trust her on this."

Any reasonable person who is also interested in getting to know the real you will respectfully accept this.

PAY SCALE

One of the most common questions I get is "who is supposed to pay?" This is a matter of personal preference. But after interviewing other successful online daters, I've found that there's a way that things will usually play out.

Date One

The male should pay. Sorry guys. Call me old-fashioned but you do have to demonstrate a bit of chivalry to win a lady's hand, at least the right lady's. Even if she contacted you, it's appropriate for you to offer to pay. Ladies, allow him to pay on this one. It doesn't mean you have to put out. It doesn't mean you have lost your female power. However, it is polite to offer to split the tab. Otherwise you may be viewed as a gold-digger. And there are many women online who are only in it for the free dinners. If the man has his wits about him, he will offer to pay.

Date Two

Both of you should offer to pay. Either of you may pick up the tab, even though some will say that it should be the person who got a free ride on the first date and others will insist that it's still the man's responsibility to continue courting the woman. If there are two activities or two checks like miniature golf and dinner or drinks, then I suggest that one person buys the first and the orher person the second.

Date Three

If someone has picked up the majority of the checks, at this point the other person should offer. If this is the fancy "win her over" dinner and especially if you suggested it, you pay. But you're not getting laid, so get that expectation out of your head, even if you paid for all three dates thus far.

Date Four

Ladies, pick this one up. Many men are offended by a woman paying for dinner, but when the check is small like a lunch or activity fee, they let it slide. You want to let them know you are interested in forming a partnership and not just taking advantage of them for free stuff.

Date Five +

By now you've figured out if you both earn the same amount or which one of you has the means to treat more times. The person with the lesser income typically treats about 25 percent of the time.

Women

If you want a chance to meet a guy who respects you, you must offer to pay some of the time. If he insists, don't get into a fight over the check. But you should make sincere attempts to cover your fair share.

Men

A woman paying for dinner once in a while is not an insult to your manhood. Allow your partner to contribute to your courtship. If you're looking for a true life partner, then you want someone who will meet you halfway. There are women online who are more interested in a free ride than meeting the love of their life. You'll weed them out with the plan above.

A Note on Dating on a Budget

I have come across a number of guys who are afraid to date online because they don't have a lot of money. You have to keep in mind that you're in control of your own dating destiny. If you choose the nicest restaurant thinking that'll impress a girl and also assume that'll be the only way she'll date you, then you have only yourself to blame. Instead, be choosy about who you want to actually meet on a date. If you can't afford martinis, meet for coffee. You don't have to pick the fanciest restaurant. It's much more informative to your date to pick a place that means something to you. The right girl will respect your effort more than the amount you're shelling out on each date. If you aren't a man of means, dating a girl who's looking for only that will end in heartbreak.

SPIN YOUR WORDS

TOPICS

Pre-determine a number of topics you'd like to discuss. Stick to things you're passionate about. Men, it can't just be sports. Women, it can't just be fashion. Everyone, it cannot be just television. Talking about media and pop culture can be an excellent entry point of common knowledge yet, once the ice is broken, you must have something else to discuss. And if the other person is not crazy for your favorite show, let it go.

There was a nervous guy on a first date who recounted the plot lines to his favorite episodes of "The Office" from start to finish. Unfortunately, his date hated the show and had scarcely seen even one episode all the way through. What's worse is that he was so amused by the wacky "Office" antics that he never picked up on her disinterest in the show. Whatever you're into, do not push it on your companion. Tee it up and if they don't take a swing at it, move on to something else.

You should not expect to hit on all of the topics that you thought of. Remember this is a date, not a job interview. But knowing that you have things to talk about if there's a lull in conversation and that there are important things you'd like a potential mate to know about you early on, can keep the date moving in the right direction.

I would hope this goes without saying, but just to make sure, debates about politics and religion have no place in a first date. It's okay to mention your religion if it's a big part of your life. But you really shouldn't get into a conversation on converting to your faith until you're more comfortable together and things look like they may be on the road to seriousness.

STORIES

What differentiates us from others are our personal experiences. You don't have to be an amazing storyteller, but everyone has a story about a defining moment or a childhood tale of bravery to share. Have a few stories in mind that you feel will give someone a window into who you are and what you're about.

I would always tell my actors this same advice in preparing them for an audition or meeting. You should not wait for the other person to lead the conversation or assume they're going to. Know what you want them to say about you before you even sit down together. However, you also need to be flexible and see how they guide the discussion.

Having a good story in your back pocket is a must for anyone, but I would suggest that daters, like actors, read the room to see the appropriateness of sharing it.

ASK THE RIGHT QUESTIONS

Being a great conversationalist is something that really can't be taught from a book. However, the best way to groom yourself to be good at talking is to be good at listening. Chances are the other person has said something you want to know more about. So ask them a direct and specific question about that.

Also, everyone loves to talk about him or herself. If you can get the other person talking about something they like, remember they may be just as nervous as you are. If they're having a good time sharing their stories, guess what? That often translates as you being more interesting. They just associate the good feelings with you, not necessarily with what they've said. But you don't want to feel they're always asking questions or that you're only talking about yourself. Check in with yourself every 10 to 15 minutes and think, "Have I asked them anything lately?" "How are they responding to my stories?" "Do I feel like I'm talking too much?" Once you have answered these questions for yourself, adjust your interaction accordingly.

Be sure to study the profile of the person you're meeting before the date. It allows you a shortcut into their life and lets them know you're interested. Do they mention something that you didn't understand? Something that intrigued you? Something that you do as well and want to talk about? The beauty of online dating is your first-date outline is already laid out for you.

BODY LANGUAGE

Body language is one of the first things that gets those tingly feelings of "chemistry" flowing, so be sure to make eye contact. Also, actively try to convey body positioning that says, "I'm listening." Avoid crossing your arms over your body in a closed stance. Always sit across from the person or at the adjacent corner to them. Men sometimes think that it might be okay to share the same side of the booth with a lady, but this is something you should wait to be invited to do. Otherwise you'll risk coming off as too forward. Wherever you position yourself make sure you can see their eyes clearly. And whatever you do, don't rest your head on your hands, lean back in your chair or check out the people who are coming and going. Even on a bad date, give the other person the consideration of being a good listener. You can look at it as practice for the next one.

THE BENEFITS OF A BAD DATE

I often say that online dating is an exercise in first dates. The pattern tends to be tiered with a number of first dates finally giving way to a handful of second and third dates. And then ultimately down to just a few who are the real deal. It's much like auditioning. You have to meet dozens of casting directors for numerous projects before the right role comes along. But if you haven't been out on the wrong auditions, you won't be prepared for the right one.

A mentor once told me it was the momentum of interviews that would build my confidence and prepare me enough to land the right job. Those other interviews were never a waste of time. Just as an audition for an actor is rarely without its merits, a bad audition—or in this case a bad date—can often teach you more about yourself than if you were able to sail through unchallenged. So even if you leave a date frustrated either because of your behavior or theirs, ask yourself, what can you learn from the experience?

TEN EASY TOPICS
TO JUMPSTART CONVERSATION

1. What kind of work do you do? What is most exciting about your job? Did you expect to be doing that when you were younger?

2. Where did you grow up? Go to school? What did you study?

3. Do you play any sports? Did you play any when you were a kid? Do you follow sports now?

4. What is your favorite hobby? What do you do when you aren't working?

5. Do you have a favorite kind of music? Musician? What's on your iPod?

6. What's your favorite kind of food? If you were trapped on a desert island with only one food to eat for the rest of your life, what would it be?

7. Have you traveled much? Where? Where do you dream about traveling to one day?

8. Are you much of a reader? Who's your favorite author? What book are you reading now?

9. Do you have any pets? Wish you had any? (This can prove useful down the road if things get serious and either of you have an allergy or aversion to pets.)

10. Do you have a big family? Grow up with cousins, aunts, uncles? Are they nearby now? What role does your family play in your life?

FOUR TOPICS THAT END A FIRST DATE CONVERSATION

1. Politics
2. Religion
3. Money
4. Old relationships

EIGHT GREAT DATE IDEAS

I highly recommend getting to know your local-event resources, whether it's from a local paper, Yelp, EventBrite or from friends on Facebook. Look for restaurants, bars and venues that host events and get on their mailing lists. That way you'll always have the inside scoop when something cool is happening there.

These ideas are only good for after date one. That's when you'll know whether you want to spend more time with this person. Unfortunately, most daters are unimaginative. Dinner and a movie has been drilled into our brains as the classic date. But with a little more effort and creativity you can go a long way toward making a great impression:

1. Festivals

Most cities hold festivals a few times a year. Like Taste of

Chicago (food), South By Southwest (music) or Montreal 's Just for Laughs Festival (comedy). Whatever you're into, there's probably a festival for it. In warm weather and bigger cities, you are lucky to have more frequent public events. These offer you an opportunity to do a lot of talking and helps give you something to talk about if the conversation dries up.

2. Get outdoors

Whether sunny or snowy, there's almost always something fun to do outside. Go for a hike. Grab a sled. Grab a pair of skis. Or a blanket on the beach.

3. Life is more romantic on a boat

If you live near a lake, ocean or river there are often great opportunities to spend some romantic time seeing the sights from a different perspective.

4. Heat things up

Amateur cooking classes have been springing up all over the place. Learning and creating something together can do wonders for intimacy.

5. Wine tasting

A number of restaurants and wine stores have begun to offer wine tastings. Dedicated wine bars are now quite popular as well. Don't like wine? Some places are now offering beer, tequila or vodka tastings. The point of these events is to expand your palate, not to get hammered. So don't make a fool of yourself.

6. Get artistic

Most cities have stores where you can paint ceramics of your choosing. They will fire your piece in a kiln and you can pick up the finished product a week later, which gives you yet another opportunity to see each other. However, this outing can get a little expensive. So you can easily create a version of this date in your backyard. Just get some supplies at an art store and let yourselves play.

7. Live performance

We've become accustomed to sitting in movie theatres without performers who can interact back. For a change, get tickets to a live theatre, music or comedy show instead. Plus, win major points for culture and creativity.

8. Get sporty

The energy of an exciting game can get even a non-sports fan in the mood. The tickets don't have to be expensive. For instance go to a college or minor league game. You can even sit in the nosebleeds. As long as you're together you'll have all you need for a good time.

How to present oneself on a date comes very easily to some, but mind-boggling for others. I never thought much about what I would put on for a date until one of my clients asked what was appropriate to wear. So I created this handy chart below which could help steer you in the right direction.The general rule is when in doubt, get a second opinion from your roommate, friend or co-worker. Family members don't make the best judges, so ask someone else if you can.

WHAT TO WEAR

Both Genders

- Go easy on visible designer labels. It's gaudy.
- Cover up because it's sexier to imagine what's underneath than to see it all.
- Make sure you match. Have a friend check your outfit if you're not sure. It's okay if you wear the same thing on multiple dates with different people, as long as you don't wear it on consecutive dates with the same person. Even if you have to email a photo of yourself in your chosen outfit to a pal, a second set of eyes for the first couple of dates is always a good idea.
- Use scents sparingly. A clean fragrance is more attractive to most people than even the fanciest cologne or perfume. Smell can be a sensitive sense for some. Be sure you don't turn them away before you even begin to speak.
- If you wear glasses every day and cannot see without them, why would you show up to a blind date actually blind, or with contacts that will have you rubbing your eyes in an hour? Invest in glasses that make you feel attractive and integrate them as part of your look.
- No holes in any article of clothing unless commissioned by the designer themselves. This is not allowed until at

least date six if you absolutely must. This includes holes in undergarments.

- Follow the pant length rule that if you can see your socks at all before you sit down then your pants are too short. Also, they are meant to be worn at your waist. Not below it. And, unless you are 80-years-old or more, definitely not above it. If you are stepping all over the bottom of your jeans when you walk, they are too long and yes, your date will notice. Here's a helpful hint: take your jeans to the tailor before they are worn out and ask them to reattach the original hem. It may cost a little more, but your jeans will look like they were made for you.

WHAT'S A WOMAN TO WEAR?

No unnecessary cleavage exposure. If you hate it when guys stare at the twins instead of looking at your eyes, then keep them inside for the day.

Dress in layers for outdoor activities. No guy likes a girl who's uncomfortable or whiny. But it's okay to just be cold enough to borrow his coat when necessary.

Don't wear shoes you can't walk in. What if he wants to take you on a leisurely stroll after dinner but you wore your four-inch Manolos? Sorry sister. That has high-maintenance written all over it.

Avoid hats for the first date. Let him see your face. Since fashion hats can be very subjective, you probably want to err on the side of caution in the beginning. Most guys would be more turned on by touchable hair.

WHAT'S A WOMAN TO WEAR?

TYPE OF DATE	FANCY DRESS	SIMPLE DRESS OR SKIRT	JEANS WITH BLOUSE/ SWEATER	TRENDY	MODEST
Drinks		X	X	X	
Dinner -Average		X		X	
Dinner - Fancy	X				X
Day Date		X	X	X	
Meeting Friends		X	X	X	
Movie			X	X	
Dancing	X	X	X	X	
Cultural Event/ Theatre	X	X			X
Game/Activity			X	X	

Pull back on the makeup, Tammy Faye. Guys like to see you and prefer not to get scared down the road when they wake up next to someone who they don't recognize without eyeliner. Sure, rouge up your cheeks a little. Put on a layer of mascara. Whatever it takes for you to feel presentable but if your look is bright eye shadow, two layers of foundation, and it takes you more than 20 minutes to prepare then dial that program back a notch.

Contrary to popular belief, a peekaboo thong hanging out of your lowrise jeans or commando flashes are not cute. Unless you're collecting cold, hard cash at the end of the night, cover it up.

HOW'S A DUDE TO DRESS?

Better to err on the side of dressing nicer than sloppier. Of course you shouldn't wear a tux and bowtie to a coffee date. But in a woman's mind, it's easier for her to picture you dressed down rather than spruced up.

Relax on the hair gel. Seriously, it will still look good. An untouchable 'do is a don't.

No chest hair showing. This should go without saying but unfortunately, it doesn't. Tuck that shag rug in your t-shirt.

It doesn't matter how big your package is, nobody wants to see it bulging through your pants. Make sure your crotch has room to breathe and your thighs too, while you're at it. And in all seriousness, if your stomach is bulging out, you do not have that size waist anymore. And that's okay. Women also come in all sizes and want men in all sizes too. Don't try to be who you are not.

HOW'S A DUDE TO DRESS?

TYPE OF DATE	BLAZER/ JACKET	BUTTON DOWN AND SLACKS	JEANS W/ SWEATER OR NICE SHIRT	METRO-SEXUAL CHIC	SUIT AND TIE
Drinks		X	X	X	
Dinner - Average	X	X		X	
Dinner - Fancy	X				X
Day Date			X	X	
Meeting Friends		X	X	X	
Movie			X	X	
Dancing		X	X	X	
Cultural Event/ Theatre	X	X		X	X
Game/Activity			X	X	

PROGRESS WORKSHEET – A

I am still confused about the online dating process and do not feel it is working for me.

O YES   O NO

I do not think my profile is attracting the right people to me or I do not think the site I am on has the selection I want.

O YES   O NO

I am nervous about meeting people online. I do not know how to be myself on a first date.

O YES   O NO

If you answered YES to two out of the above three questions you're doing just fine. If you keep going at this pace you will find someone with whom you want to spend more time. Just stick with it. If you answered NO to two or more, please proceed to the next worksheet.

PROGRESS WORKSHEET – B

I am happy with the frequency of dates I'm going on.

O YES O NO

I am satisfied with the selection of mates that I have found on my current dating site.

O YES O NO

I have enjoyed going on dates even if they have not progressed into long term relationships

O YES O NO

If you answered NO to any of the above questions, read on. The answers you need may be below. If you cannot get yourself back on track and need additional attention, check the website for other available services.

GETTING STUCK
IN YOUR OWN WEB

Everyone gets to a point in online dating when the initial excitement wears off and it becomes time to really get down to work. Here are some common obstacles when you might feel like giving up and my suggestions on how help to push yourself through the discouragement.

You Never Get Responses to Your Emails

The most common complaint I hear from new clients is about the low number of replies they receive. Many assume that everyone else's inboxes are flooded with potential dates and that they've failed at the game after as little as two or four weeks. They say, "Online dating doesn't work for me" and give up on all of the momentum they have built through sending messages, being active online and conducting searches in new and inventive ways.

An average response rate is about 10 to 20 percent for most online daters. The stunningly gorgeous can see response rates closer to 50 percent depending on the site, but even they don't bat 1,000. Keep these stats in mind. This means that you have to send 10 messages to get one or two responses back. The techniques in this book have helped singles see an improvement in responses, but even so, daters need to be persistent to improve their chances of finding true love online.

If you find yourself getting discouraged by a few unanswered emails, the most constructive reaction isn't to sign off and swear that online dating is hopeless, but rather to examine if you're doing everything that you can to be successful. Take another good look at your profile. Does it truly represent who you are and the kind of person you want to meet? Or are you saying what you think someone would want to hear? Look at the people you're contacting. Are you being too narrow in your selections?"

To break out of the slump, send some emails to people you otherwise wouldn't reach out to. Do you see something in their profile that catches your eye? Go ahead and write them even if they aren't the exact height or profession you've had in mind. You have to put yourself out there in a new way. Never hold yourself back from sending an email to someone because you think they wouldn't give you the time of day. It's always said that in the perfect relationship, you both feel that you're the lucky one, so don't be afraid to aim high with your selections.

COUNTLESS FIRST DATES THAT NEVER RESULT IN A SECOND

Feeling disappointed by having continual introductory conversations that never progress into more is perfectly common. As I said earlier, think of online dating as an exercise in first dates. It's really just traditional matchmaking on speed, and best of all, you get to be your own matchmaker. The result is that in today's world you know more quickly if someone is right for you. Take the pressure off of yourself to find "the one" and look at each person and each date individually, not as an indicator of the future to come. This might also ease some of the tension that you didn't realize you were bringing to your dates.

You Went on the "Perfect Date" and Never Heard from Them Again

Online dating can be a bitch. Here's the dose of love being a two-way street that your grandma was always talking about. Just because you thought you had the most perfect union and saw yourself having children with them after only one date doesn't mean they felt the same way. You can't force it. If someone doesn't seem interested in you after only date one, they're really not worth fighting for. Turn that attention to something positive like finding more dates.

When You See All the Same Faces Online

If you're on a specialized site you may be swimming in a pool that is too shallow. Even if you're looking for a specific quality, try a free search on a larger site. You may be surprised who you find. Also, if you've been doing your homework you may be familiar with all of the faces just because you've been investigating the site thoroughly. In that case it's also a good idea to take a look at another site. No need to pay the money and commit. But if you do a free search and like who you find, chances are there are more you'll like if you do sign up.

If you're in a larger site and you've been working at it regularly but are still bored, try shaking up your search criteria. Look in a nearby city. Don't see anyone you like? Try some place further away where you have sometimes fantasized about living. Or, perhaps you've only dated people of your same ethnic background. You have nothing against dating someone of another ethnicity, it's just you haven't really thought about it. Well, try a search, and see if anyone catches your eye.

TAKE A BREAK

It takes a lot of energy to date online and get results. If you're working too hard and getting burned out, take a vacation from the internet. Work hard, play hard, but put a clock on it. Rather than saying, "I'm going to sign on and see if I meet someone a different way." Give yourself a timed break. "I'm going to take this month off and come back after the holidays." When you return, you will feel refreshed, encouraged and optimistic. You'll see new faces. And you'll have the opportunity to reset any habits that weren't serving you. When I was online dating, I usually would do three months on, then take one month off. I always felt much better and was able to set more dates when I came back fresh to my dating project. With many sites, you get a better rate if you sign up for three to six months at a time, and I do encourage signing up for a longer membership than one month. The first month is usually awash when you factor in the time it takes to get your profile just how you want it and the process of sorting through possible suitors. In many cases, if you've signed up for a full year, even if you take a month or two off, you'll still end up saving money over a month-to-month plan.

DIFFICULT CHOICES

I often hear from shy daters who always take things one step at a time with one person at a time. Then they suddenly find

PROGRESS WORKSHEET – C

I have met someone special. I don't know if they are "the one" or not but I am currently spending at least one night a week with them.

○ YES ○ NO

I have met a couple of people I like but I am not sure who I like better.

○ YES ○ NO

I am really having fun dating online. I thought I'd be ready to settle down but now that I see what it's like, I just want to keep meeting new people.

○ YES ○ NO

themselves caught between two or more great options.

Online daters, realize that you are dating—or at least talking to—multiple people. That is the nature of online dating. It's perfectly acceptable to see multiple people at once as long as you are upfront about being out there and make it clear that you are not yet exclusive with anyone.

When things start to get serious with one person though, you need to be upfront with the other(s). It isn't fair to keep someone in your back pocket. If they're not interesting enough to you to be your Number One, you owe it to them to find another person who will. The key to all of this is honesty. As long as your dates know where they stand with you, your part of the bargain is upheld.

When you do break things off with person Number Two,

however, you should avoid mentioning that there's someone else. If you make it about the two of you not being a match, they will tend to take the news better and you are more likely to avoid the clingy dumpee constantly coming back to see if things have finally gone south with the other person.

Alternatively, you may find that over time neither is right for you and that's perfectly normal too. I urge you not to stay in a dating situation that you know is not an ideal fit. It's unfair to the other person if they really like you and it only keeps you from putting your attention toward finding your right match.

Differences

She shares the same hobbies as you. You both love the same bands. You grew up in the same state. You discovered you had several friends in common but never met one another until you both went onine. Everything is perfect except one thing. What to do about it depends on how big the thing is:

Religion

This depends on the importance of religion to both you and your partner. If it's essential you raise your children to be of a certain religion, share this with your mate when things seem to be getting serious. They may be of a different religion but not have strong feelings about raising the kids to follow in their faith. Or they may want to try exposing the children to both. Who knows? They may be open to converting to your religion or joining your church. This issue is only a deal-breaker if you choose for it to be. It's possible to have a strong relationship with differing religious views as long as you respect one another's beliefs and don't make an attempt to change the other's point of view.

Children

This subject also depends on how strongly you and your partner feel. But this isn't something that usually changes once someone has firmly made up their mind. So it's not something that should be brushed under the rug if you have strong opposing views. You should discuss both adopting and having kids biologically, as that could elicit a different response.

If one person has kids, those children need to always be a part of the discussion. If your partner has a child and waits a while before introducing you, do not become upset. Dealing with children in new relationships is very tricky and you must respect that your partner needs to find the right time and place to introduce you. If you love the person, you must also love their child, as they will always be the biggest part of their life. Whatever you do, do not make a competition between you and their children.

If you already have children, you should let your date know and explain the way in which you're involved in their lives—such as primary caretaker, weekends or long distance parenting. Just be sure that you are not making the date all about your kids. That's usually not perceived as very sexy.

Social Issues and Politics

There are a number of successful couples who differ on political issues. The key is to keep the discussion out of the bedroom or other intimate encounters and to make sure those debates stay more intellectual than emotional. Also, you'll need to make sure that you have a group of mutual friends who balance out the issue. And never allow one partner to get bullied about their point of view. If you can't do this, you either need to avoid talking about these topics entirely or find someone else who you see eye to eye with.

Be wary of becoming a date perfectionist who's always searching for that one chance to say, "See? They weren't perfect, I'll never meet Mr. Right." The right person is not perfect and neither are you. But in actuality, the right person makes you question things, helps you to evolve and learn to compromise.

DIFFICULT CONVERSATIONS

You like them. They seem to like you. So it may be time for "the talk." It's always a little awkward to have, but the two of you need to know that you're on the same page. It doesn't need to be a high school exchange of "will you be my boyfriend?" But I would recommend finding out if you're exclusive or if you're continuing to keep your profile active.

Once you acknowledge that there's no one else in the picture, take your profile down. You're in the right to ask your partner take down their profile as well. It's entirely reasonable to say, "I'm deleting my profile tomorrow. It's important to me that you take yours down as well."

Often online daters want to keep someone in their back pocket. No one likes to be dumped or disappointed. But if you truly want to give a relationship a shot at working, you can't keep that other door open. You can always go back online and re-post if things don't work out. However if you're really interested in someone, you need to be focused on just them. Inevitably, if your profile stays up, you'll get another message or see some selections from the site that catch your eye and start questioning your choice of partner. That's not fair to you or to them.

Sometimes you get beyond "the talk" without even realizing it. If it becomes natural to refer to this person as your boyfriend or girlfriend when they're not around, try doing it when they're present. Based on the reaction you get, you should be able to infer what their perspective is. Once you have labeled yourself a couple, there's no more scanning online for others until you've taken things as far as you can with this person.

Some people don't like labels and may not want to put those very words to it. That's fine, but you should know whether or not you're still keeping a toe in the online dating pool or whether you're giving this relationship your total focus. There's no set amount of time in which this happens. I had a client who said she knew by her second date that they wanted to be exclusive. He's with the man she ultimately married. My husband and I went about eight weeks before bridging the topic. One or two months seems to be the average, but faster or slower doesn't make it any more right or wrong.

I would say that if one of you is not ready to commit after six months, something is probably not working and I'd recommend you revisit the list of qualities your right mate will possess. See if this person truly matches up.

MOVING IN

I have one major condition on the moving-in issue: Make sure that you have a candid discussion about what co-habitation means. I've seen many people move in for convenience or without having a mutual understanding of what it means for the relationship, only to then have the relationship end poorly and awkwardly when one person not only had to find a new mate, but also a new place to call home. Unless you really have discussions like, "this means we're moving toward marriage" or "I need help with rent, but I don't intend to get married" or "I don't like to live alone," then you're not ready to move in. If you're afraid of getting your feelings hurt by the answer, just know that you'll get the answer eventually, but it'll likely be harder to hear later when you have more invested. If you're not sure of your intentions, step back and take time to figure them out before making a decision as big as co-habitation.

MEETING THE FRIENDS

At times this can be more important than meeting mom and dad. This is because your mate will take the opinion of their friends to heart more than that of their parents. Also, many singles do not live as close to their parents as they did in previous generations, so the friend circle takes the important role of supporting the individual in the way that biological family units often did in the past.

Luckily, you're likely to have more in common with friends than parents so your chances of success should be good if you and your partner are truly a good match.

Here are some guidelines:

1. It's a good idea to meet more than one friend at a time. If you just meet the best friend, all of the pressure is going to be on you and there may even be a sense of competition for your man or woman's attention. You may also end up feeling like the third wheel on a bicycle if they launch into a conversation about an old story or a shared experience that they had. Three is just an awkward number, so try to avoid it.

2. Don't be a wallflower. If your mate brings you to a party where you don't know anyone, make an effort to socialize and don't feel like you need to be hanging at their side the whole time. A strong couple can exist both apart and together. Your date will be impressed if you can strike up a conversation on your own and allow them some alone time to catch up with their bud. Just don't end up in a dark corner talking to the most attractive person of the opposite sex.

3. Don't get hammered. You may have succeeded in not letting your nerves on get the best of you on the first date, but meeting friends can be intimidating. Try to think of this meeting or party as the first date with your partner's friends. Don't do anything to turn them off or embarrass yourself this early on.

MEETING THE PARENTS

Meeting the parents is a blind date in and of itself. You've heard a lot about them. Maybe seen pictures of them. You've been told what they're like or what their favorite hobbies are. But that doesn't mean you have a sense of how to interact with them. Following just a few simple guidelines can make it an enjoyable experience:

1. Don't try to make them like you. If you are trying too hard you'll have the opposite effect. Instead, they'll be more impressed to find you honest and genuine as a potential partner.

2. If possible, meet them in a neutral location for the first introduction. If you're meeting them at their home you're already on their territory. You'll feel more comfortable if you can first meet them in a place where you can be yourself and where you aren't already working against a family shorthand. There are little things in a home that can get you into trouble like sitting in someone else's chair at the dinner table, making the wrong comment on artwork or using the wrong bathroom or towel. All of these added pressures only keep you from getting to actually knowing them person-to-person instead of just as their child's date or partner.

3. Remember things your significant other told you about their parents and actively ask questions about them.

But don't make it an interview like this:

SALLY: *John tells me you love to golf.*

MR. MILLER: *Oh, yes, I've been to all the biggest courses around the country.*

SALLY: *Where have you been?*

MR. MILLER: *All over, Hiltonhead, Palm Springs, Hawaii.*

SALLY: *That's great. Sounds like you've traveled a lot.*

MR. MILLER: *Oh yeah, I've actually been to all seven continents.*

SALLY: *Wow. Neat. Can you pass the potatoes?*

There were several openings in which Sally could have inserted her opinion or taken the conversation in a direction that she was more comfortable. The trick is you need to find a way to connect the conversation back to something about you. Here's an example of how Sally could've taken a more active role in the conversation:

SALLY: John tells me you love to golf.

MR. MILLER: Oh, yes, I've been to all the biggest courses around the country.

SALLY: Have you been to Castle Pines? That's only a couple of hours from where I grew up.

MR. MILLER: I haven't, but I've heard it's one of the best in the country.

SALLY: My dad loves that one! He's a big Nicklaus fan.

MR. MILLER: Do you golf with your dad?

SALLY: I tried a couple of times but I'm not that good. I'm definitely open to tips from a golf pro.

MR. MILLER: I'm no expert but I'd be happy to take you guys out to the range sometime.

In this scenario, Sally did several things right. Not only did she find a way to connect her personal story to something Mr. Miller was excited about, but she also gave him a bit of an ego boost by acknowledging what he was good at by calling him a 'golf pro'.

It's all about finding common ground for the first meeting and then letting that bond the two of you on a similar level. Otherwise, if you over-elevate your partner's parents it will be harder for them to bond with you and see you as compatible with their family.

CALLING IT OFF

You have to look at finding your ideal mate as your job, your mission that you've chosen to accept. Have you ever been so focused on the person you're dating that you never stepped back to think, "Is this actually my best fit? Is this person my soul mate?" And even when you know you want out of the relationship, often you don't know where to begin the discussion. Have you ever bought a pair of pants that looked great online and then found they fit terribly when they arrived? I you want a refund, you have to take the initiative and send the pants back.

As much as we'd like for everyone who looks good on paper to be as great as we imagine them to be, sometimes we realize that over time our vision of the relationship is better than it is in actuality. Knowing when a relationship is not serving us is one of the most frightening, and also one of the most liberating, things each of us can do. I can't tell you when that is, but I can say that when you know, you know. Usually people ignore their inner voice that tells them it's over. Then they spend months going back and forth with the hope that fate will intervene and end it for them or miraculously turn their mate into the person they'd hoped they could be.

First, you have to remember that it's always your option to call it quits and it's actually your responsibility to do so if the other person isn't your right partner. The same is true for your mate.

The process is different depending on where you each are in the relationship's life. Relationships are complex so there's not a

RELATIONSHIP SCORECARD

Do you have more than 1 fight in a week?

O YES   O NO

Do most of those arguments end with you apologizing?

O YES   O NO

Do you find yourself compromising for your partner often?

O YES   O NO

Do you spend more time with their friends than yours?

O YES   O NO

Do they ever insult you in front of other people (even in jest)?

O YES   O NO

Do you have differing opinions on a major issue (marriage, children, religion) and avoid discussing it entirely?

O YES   O NO

Do they ever pay more attention to another person or object when you're around (videogames, computer, reading, television, pets)?

O YES   O NO

If you answered YES to four or more of these questions it's probably time to sit down and ask yourself, "Is my relationship serving me?"

one-size-fits-all answer on when to leave one. Below is a scorecard that might help you see when there may be a disconnect between what you have and what you want.

Go back to your original list of qualities you're looking for in a partner. Are you with that person or did you allow physical attraction—or something else—sway you? Make a list of the positives and negatives in your relationship. If that list is unbalanced, you should start considering the reasons why. Everyone deserves to be in the right relationship. Staying with someone who you know is wrong for you is only keeping both of you from fulfilling that destiny.

THREE DATES OR LESS

Yes, the rule of three strikes again. You will notice that this is when the cracks begin to show. Remember that you may not be the only person your partner has seen in those three dates. After a mere three dates the emotional investment of both parties should be relatively small, so it shouldn't be too hard for you to throw that trout back in the sea and keep fishing.

I always recommend communicating your intentions as soon as you set them. When you don't at least give a "sorry it's not working out for me" email or call, you leave that door open for them to try and it open again. As long as you're direct and honest about your feelings, no one can fault you. But make sure you take the responsibility upon yourself rather than throwing it on them.

Here's some sample phrasings. Feel free to put this conversation in your own words: "I've enjoyed our time together, but I have to be honest that I'm not feeling like this is a fit. I wish you lots of luck on meeting someone special." The actual wording should be as you would say it. The key, though, is that no language is ambiguous, nothing said is accusatory and that the blame for it not working out is placed on yourself.

After three dates, this information really should be communicated in a phone call, rather than through email out of respect for the other person.

With online dating it's possible to make a clean break as you won't have to see each other at parties by mutual friends or at work every day or talk to their mom when you run into her at the grocery store. As long as you end things in a cordial way, you're free and clear to start dating someone else right away.

UP TO EIGHT DATES

This gets trickier. Now you have invested some time, but you still aren't fully connected to this person yet.

Here's a scenario. Let's call the couple Jenny and Sam. Jenny is stoked about Sam. He thinks she's hot, but finds her incessant talking to be annoying—very annoying. They went on their last date four days ago and Sam hasn't called since. He thought she would get the hint. But alas, non-communication is not a hint. It's a question mark or worse, a fill in the blank. So Jenny calls him for the second time since the date....

JENNY: *Hey Sam, what's going on?*
SAM: Not much...(insert small talk here)
JENNY: (insert small talk reply)...So what's up for Saturday

night? Are we going out again this week?

SAM: *I actually have plans with my buddy Rick, but I'm really glad you called.*

JENNY: *Oh yeah, why is that?*

Right now Sam is thinking, "Why didn't she get the hint?" But you see, there is no hint. If the other person thinks it's going well they'll come up with a myriad of other excuses as to why you haven't called. Sam just needs to cut to the chase and be direct.

SAM: *Well, you know we haven't talked in a few days and in that time I've been doing some thinking.*

JENNY: *Thinking about us?*

Jenny still isn't getting what's coming because in her mind she has told herself an entirely different story about how her relationship with Sam is going. So Sam has to spell it out. This doesn't mean that Jenny is stupid, it's just that her expectations were different so she's viewed Sam's actions through a different prism.

SAM: *Yes, actually. I've been thinking you're really interesting and I've had a great time getting to know you, but I have to be honest that I'm not feeling this is a match.*

JENNY: *If I'm so great then why wouldn't you want to keep seeing me?*

Inevitably Jenny is going to be hurt and this will probably manifest itself as anger. That's okay. Sam just needs to stay the course.

SAM: *It's hard to put into words, but something is missing for me and I don't want to keep you from finding the right guy for you because unfortunately, it's not me.*

Sam's directness doesn't allow Jenny to manipulate his decision. Honesty about your feelings is really the best policy. No one can argue with your feelings because they belong to you and you alone.

JENNY: *I see. Well, can we be friends at least?*
SAM: *I'm afraid right now that might confuse things. Maybe down the road. But for now I don't think that's a good idea.*

Do not leave that door open. Friends will inevitably be friends with benefits which will then become a confusing sort of dating situation again.

JENNY: *Okay Sam. Well, I appreciate you being honest with me.*
SAM: *Thanks. I appreciate your honesty as well. Good luck. I really wish you the best.*

We all know it's not always that easy and often Jenny will insert a guilt trip in between those lines. But keep to the script especially when the other person strays. The key moments are the ones when you own your feelings and clearly express your intentions. If your intention is not to date this person, don't be vague. It may hurt their feelings for a while. But if you lead them on or allow room for them to try to change your mind, they probably will and you'll likely end up with an even bigger issue on your hands when you want to break it off later.

When The Dump is on You

Conversely, when you are the dumpee you shouldn't take it personally. As I said before, it's the other person's duty to allow you the space to find the right one for yourself, too. So rather than looking at it as failure, look at it as an opportunity to find someone even better.

How to Know You've Found "the One"

This is one question that really does not have an answer. I can say for myself that as I got to know my husband, I just knew he was right in the same way that I just knew when someone was wrong for me.

Petty bickering doesn't rear its ugly head. Sure you don't agree on everything, but the idea of being at odds with your partner might even turn your stomach. Your greatest joy will come from seeing your partner happy. Your selfish voices will quiet and suddenly decisions will only be able to be made based on "we" instead of based on "me." You begin to realize that you're no longer sweating the small stuff and that your future has a deeper meaning to you than any chance to "be proven right" does.

People you once found attractive, who only ended up being the wrong kind of person for you, will start to look the way you needed to see them in the first place. And the idea of being with anyone else will feel foreign.

You'll begin to see past the present and into the future. Sure,

I wrote my first name next to past boyfriends' surnames just to see how it looked, but when I met my husband-to-be I could see a future world beyond the name. I thought of my children's names instead of my own.

I often hear about people being hesitant to marry and being unsure if the person they're with is "the one." In fact, I often expected myself to be one of those people. In my vision of the future before I met him, I saw only me and my career with some casual romantic relationships and maybe a dog. But he flipped the script that I had written for my life. The moment when he he proposed there was only one thing I could think of to say: "Of course."

Everyone deserves that feeling. You deserve it. Now you owe that to yourself to go find it.

Go Out and Get What You Want

If you ask 100 couples how they met you will probably hear 100 unique and interesting stories. Though I met my husband online and about 20 of those other people you ask would probably have too, I look at online dating as one tool in your toolbox. However, once you begin online dating, you'll find that you see mate possibilities all around you, and thanks to your blind dating skills, you may also find it easier to communicate with strangers. Online dating not only changed my life by leading to a wonderful marriage and a beautiful daughter, but it completely shifted the way I thought about myself and infused me with the confidence to go after ANYTHING that I wanted in life.

In my coaching sessions with clients I encourage them to

look at the full dating spectrum and acknowledge the missed opportunities they've had to meet the perfect partner. Staying focused on your dating life is not always easy. Work, family and ego often get in the way, but if you're dedicated to dating like it's YOUR JOB and willing to make changes to the patterns that haven't delievered the results you've wanted in the past, you can find the relationship of your dreams.

If you are motivated to find love and want additional support, make it happen and let me help. I'd love to see you in a webinar or workshop—and from there, walking down the aisle. Please visit my website to share your experiences and success stories for other daters to learn from. There, you'll also find other resources to get you that perfect partner.

See you online at *www.DearMrsD.com.*

ENDORSEMENTS
for "SPIN YOUR WEB"

"I have seen Damona in-action…on the set of my show. She is so passionate about helping people find love. It's clearly her calling, and she's changing the way people view online dating. She is confident, personable, and full of wisdom—It's been a pleasure working with Damona."

–Mechelle Collins, Executive Producer, *The Millionaire Matchmaker*

"Dear Mrs D decodes the sometimes overwhelming world of online dating by providing accessible advice singles can use. As a regular and valued contributor to JMag, the online magazine for JDate.com, Dear Mrs D helps singles sort through the questions and issues that arise related to dating—with the mission of helping people find their match!"

–Editors of *JMag*, the online magazine for *JDate.com*

"The perfect primer for internet dating. Use this book to get the most out of your internet dating experience and learn Internet dating netiquette. Damona gives you the groundwork to prepare quickly for a successful idating experience. She helps you ask the right questions, choose the best site, and avoid pitfalls both online and offline."

– Mark Brooks, CEO of *Online Personals Watch*

"Damona's book is chock full of tangible advice for singles —not general statements. You get a true action plan for how to "market" yourself for online dating success. I love it!"

–Adele Testani, Co-Founder of *HurryDate*

"Having met her husband online, Damona offers clear, thoughtful advice on how to turn your dating life around."

–Julie Spira, bestselling author, online dating expert, and CEO of *CyberDatingExpert.com*

Made in the USA
Lexington, KY
20 May 2013